# Life on Purpose

## 30 Days of Listening to the One Who Calls You

### KATY EPLING

ISBN 978-1-7362592-0-7 (Paperback)
ISBN 978-1-7362592-1-4 (eBook)

# CONTENTS

# INTRODUCTION

Welcome, friend. Thanks for taking this little journey with me. I hope the next 30 days bring you clarity and confidence. This concept of purpose and calling is a hard one, but important. In fact, let me tell you a little bit about why I wrote this journal.

Honestly, I have lost track of the number of times in my life I have looked around and thought, "Why am I even here?" It amazes me how often I flounder, wondering what my purpose could possibly be.

I have found that there tend to be two times in life when we lose our sense of purpose: when life is *ordinary* and when it is *extraordinary*. Think about it... When our lives seem mundane, the same day in and day out, we might think, "Am I actually doing anything of value? Do I really need to be here?" And when something extraordinary happens—parenthood, a job change, a pandemic—we can get completely thrown off-course and feel rudderless, wondering how we got here and what on earth we're supposed to be doing.

When we lose our sense of direction, we need a compass to point us to true north. And just in case I need to spell it out for you, God is our true north, and His Word is our compass. Although the Bible's primary purpose is to tell who God is, it also has quite a bit to say about who we are and why we're here—that, my friend, is identity and purpose.

So let's take some time to immerse ourselves daily in God's Word. Let's spend time with the One who created us, the very One who gives us purpose. Let's remember who we are and Whose we are.

My prayer—and yes, my friend, I am praying for you as you read this—is that you will be built upon a firm foundation so that you can withstand the storms of life. I pray that the pages of this journal give you space to spend time with God, to root yourself in him. And ultimately, I pray the words of Paul:

> *So here's what I want you to do, God helping you: Take your everyday, ordinary life—your sleeping, eating, going-to-work, and walking-around life—and place it before God as an offering.*
>
> *Romans 12:1 (The Message)*

# USING THE JOURNAL

Before you begin, let's talk about what you can expect from the next 30 or so pages. This book was written to be a journal-meets-devotional-meets-Bible-study, but that took up too much space on the cover page. This is written to help you dig into God's Word and understand what he says about who you are and why you're here. He is, after all, the one who made you, so he probably has a few thoughts on the matter.

First (and I cannot stress this enough), **spend some time in prayer**. Praise God for who he is and for meeting you there. Listen, friend, this is the God of the universe, and he is happily sitting down each day with you. That is pretty incredible. Ask him to open your eyes to what he has for you in his Word today. As James reminds us, "If any of you lacks wisdom, let him ask God, who gives generously to all without reproach, and it will be given him" (1:5). And honestly, don't just say "amen" and move on. This entire process should be bathed in prayer—beginning, middle, and end.

Now that your heart is ready, go to that day's entry and **read a passage of Scripture**. If you don't have a Bible, that's OK! We live in such an amazing technological age that you can read one on your phone or your computer for free! Several great websites/apps exist, but I personally use YouVersion (bible.com). As you read, take your time. This isn't just a step to get through, this is the most important part of what you will do each day! Read it a couple of times. Read it in different translations. Don't just read, study. (And if you want some additional Bible study tips, you'll find them at the end of the book!)

Next, you'll find a **brief summary** from me, explaining the main point we are focusing on for the day. I want to emphasize the word brief here. The goal of this journal is not for you to hear my thoughts on the Bible, but to help you better listen to his voice for yourself. Read the couple of sentences I wrote, and then maybe go back and re-read the passage one more time with that topic/focus in mind.

Now you're ready to **journal**. I have provided a few questions for you to ponder that relate to the day's topic, but don't feel obligated or limited by those. This is your space to process what God has laid on your heart, not mine. Write as much or as little as you wish. Answer the questions or don't. You can even use that space to write out a prayer for the day.

As you may have surmised (because, my friend, you are smart and I believe in you), this journal contains 30 entries. Each one is numbered, so you can walk through them day-by-day. But guess what: this is your journal! So if day 6 catches your eye first, go for it! And if day 18 seems like it would be better on a different day, skip it! Just one word of advice on this, though: if you're tempted to skip a day because it seems too hard, don't. If the Holy Spirit is whispering you to dig in and your insecurities are pushing to give up, don't let the negativity win. Remember: what you feed grows. Each time we listen to God's voice instead of our enemy's and push through the hard, it gets a little bit easier to do it again the next time, and the next time, and the next.

Also, I wrote 30 entries so readers could complete this journey in a month. But once again, I am not the boss of you. You might take one month and walk all the way through it, or you might use it Monday through Friday and complete it in 6 weeks, or maybe you just do this each Monday morning (or Tuesday or Saturday...) and really take your time with it. It is completely up to you. You're not doing it wrong. (I feel the need to emphasize this encouragement for all of the rule followers like myself out there.)

However you use this journal, make sure you are carrying it with you all day long—not the physical pages, but the concepts. Think and pray throughout the day about what you read in God's Word, what he laid on your heart, what he is teaching you about him and about his purpose for you.

Because you, my friend, were

*created on purpose, for a purpose.*

Journal

# *Part 1*

## SHIFTING OUR PERSPECTIVE

When we read the Bible, we often want to rush to personal application: What does this say about me?" And while God is definitely teaching us about who we are and our place in the world, that's not the primary focus of Scripture. When we come to God's Word, our first question should be, "What does this teach me about God?" So yes, over the next 30 days, we will look at what the Bible teaches about our purpose... but first we need to understand that it's not really about us. We need to gain a right perspective of who God is, and then we can explore what he says about who we are.

*Day 1*

# THE FIRST QUESTION WE SHOULD ASK

**Read:** Psalm 139

**Consider:**

Psalm 139 is a passage many of us use to see our worth. We read verses 13 and 14 and think, "Wow, I'm really special!" But when we read the psalm as a whole, we see that it is isn't really about us at all—it's about the greatness of God. In order to have a right view of ourselves and our purpose, we must first have a right view of God and how much bigger—infinitely bigger—he is than us.

Similarly, when we read Scripture, we often rush to application. We want to know, "What does this say about/to me?" But our first question should be, "What does this teach me about God?" With that in mind, for the first few days of our study, we will take this familiar psalm and try to gain a new perspective.

**Journal:**

1.  What would you say is the main point of this psalm? What is the author trying to convey?

2.  What attributes of God do you see as you read Psalm 139? Make a list!

3.  What do you hope to gain by the end of these thirty days? Spend some time in prayer about what you would like to learn from this journey and jot down your hopes and goals. Be as specific as you can.

# KEY CHARACTERISTICS OF GOD

**Read:** Psalm 139

**Consider:**

As we read this psalm, we see some key characteristics of God:

1. He is all-knowing (vv. 1-4). God knows us inside and out—he even knows our words before we even think of them!

2. He is beyond time (vs. 5). He goes ahead of us, he is behind us, redeeming our past, and he has his hand on us right here and now.

3. He is beyond our understanding (vv. 6, 17). We cannot even begin to grasp his knowledge.

4. He is beyond space (vv. 7-12). God is everywhere. No height or depth is so great that he cannot see us.

**Journal:**

1. Using the list above and your own list of God's characteristics that you made yesterday, write about the ways you have seen them in your own life. When have you known that God was "hemming you in, behind and before"? When have you realized that your understanding is limited compared to his?

2. As you look at the vastness of God's abilities and understanding, how does that affect the way you then look at yourself? What does it mean if THAT God chose to create you?

# CHANGING OUR FOCUS

**Read:** Psalm 139

**Consider:**

Although verses 13-16 are often used to remind us of our worth, they are actually there to create a contrast. God is infinite—he is the Creator, large enough to knit us together, powerful enough to know all of our days before we even take a breath. We are tiny by comparison—the creation, able to be fully known, the breadth of our lives determined before we are born.

**Journal:**

1. How do these verses change the way you see God?

2. In what ways do these verses humble you?

3. In what ways do they encourage you?

# Day 4

## GOD WANTS YOU

**Read:** Psalm 139

**Consider:**

God knew every single one of your days before you took a single breath. Can you believe that? It is hard to fully grasp, but it's true. That also means that he knew every victory and defeat, every struggle you would face, every negative trait—and still he chose you. He made you. From his throne, he knitted you together, looked at the days of your life, and said, "Yes, I want you."

**Journal:**

1.  Have you felt that God could no longer use you because of mistakes you've made? Have you ever faced a sudden change in life that you didn't see coming? How does it make you feel to know that God saw all of your days and still wanted you?

2.  What are some ways God has used your mistakes or your unexpected circumstances for his glory? What in your life right now are you hoping he can redeem and use?

# GOD'S PLAN WILL NOT BE THWARTED

**Read:** Psalm 57:1-3, 138:7-8

**Consider:**

In both of these psalms, David is facing trials—in fact, in Psalm 57 we're told he's hiding in a cave! He calls out to God for help, but he is not shaken. He remains confident in God's faithfulness and power. In both psalms he declares that God will fulfill his purpose for David. This tells us three things:

1. God is the one doing the work! David doesn't say, "Don't worry, God! I'm still working at fulfilling your purpose for me!" He just lays his life—and purpose—in God's hands.

2. God's plans will not be thwarted. Whatever you're going through right now, it is not stopping God from fulfilling his purpose for you.

3. Trials and suffering aren't a detour from God's plan for our lives. They are part of his plan. When we trust God in the midst of our hard circumstances, we give him the opportunity to show his power—to us and everyone around us—which is absolutely part of his purpose for us!

**Journal:**

1. As David calls out to God for mercy and reminds himself of God's faithfulness, it seems odd that he would mention purpose in the midst of it. Why do you think he brought that topic up in these verses?

2. How does life look different when we are the ones trying to fulfill our purpose versus trusting that God will fulfill his purpose for us?

3. How does knowing that God's plan for your purpose includes the trials and pain you'll go through change your perspective of your circumstances?

# *Part 2*

## THE SIGNIFICANT LIFE

We all want to feel like we are significant. Unfortunately, our culture tells us that our significance is found in the number and size of our accomplishments... but no matter how much we accomplish, it never seems to be quite enough.

God's Word, though, tells a different story. He doesn't ask us to earn our significance. He doesn't require us to mark off a checklist. His measure of significance looks entirely different from what the world tries to tell us. Of course, that doesn't mean God's way is always easy, but it's far simpler than we try to make it.

# WALK IN A WORTHY MANNER

**Read:** Ephesians 4:1-7

**Consider:**

For a long time, Ephesians 4:1 weighed on me. Here is Paul, literally a prisoner for his faith, admonishing his readers to "walk in a manner worthy of the calling to which you have been called." That seems like a tall order—impossible, honestly! How can anything I do possibly measure up to what Paul did for Christ? What could I ever accomplish that would be worthy of my calling?

Fortunately, Paul explains exactly what a worthy walk looks like... and what he says might surprise you. He doesn't tell his readers to accomplish big things or reach a certain amount of people for Christ or be big and loud enough to be thrown into jail. Instead, he tells us that a worthy walk is marked by humility, gentleness, patience, love, and unity.

We want to complicate our call, to make it something big and elusive. But ultimately, God calls us to something much simpler—though not necessarily easy. Humility, gentleness, patience... all things I strive for, but I still miss the mark more often than I care to admit. However, when I take my eyes off of my works and focus them on Christ, these are the qualities that grow in me and enable me to walk in my calling.

**Journal:**

1. Before you studied this passage, how would you have defined a "worthy walk"? How has today's study changed that?

2. Does changing the definition of a worthy walk make you feel more or less intimidated? In what ways is it easier? In what ways is it harder?

3. The hallmarks of a worthy walk, according to Paul, are humility, gentleness, patience, love, and unity. Which of those do you think describe you? Where do you feel like you need to grow?

## EVERYDAY, ORDINARY LIFE

**Read:** Romans 12:1-8

**Consider:**

As in the passage before this one, Paul's words at first feel a little overwhelming. What could possibly make my life "acceptable" to God? How could I ever do anything big or important enough? But in The Message, Eugene Peterson writes Romans 12:1 this way: "So here's what I want you to do, God helping you: Take your everyday, ordinary life—your sleeping, eating, going-to-work, and walking-around life—and place it before God as an offering." It's not about *what* we do, but about *how* we do it. Remember, God cares far more about who we are than what we do.

**Journal:**

1.  How can you place your "everyday, ordinary life" before God as an offering? What might that look like?

2.  Is it hard for you to think that giving God your everyday life is enough? Why do you think that is?

## AN OFFERING TO GOD BECAUSE OF WHAT HE HAS DONE

**Read:** Romans 12:1-8

**Consider:**

When we see words like "therefore" in the Bible, we should take note! The author isn't making an isolated point, but is drawing a conclusion based on something he already said. In this case, Paul has just spent the first 11 chapters laying out the entire story of God and his people, explaining man's fallenness, our need for a savior, and God's provision—first to Israel through the covenants, then to the entire world through Jesus. Go back and read Romans 11:33-36 to get a picture of just how incredible Paul thinks the gospel really is—what an absolute gift God has given us who believe. Therefore—in light of God's goodness and mercy and the plan He has been putting together from the dawn of creation to draw us into relationship with him—we should take our lives, everything we say and do, and place them before God as an offering.

**Journal:**

1.  How does reading the concluding verses of chapter 11, and thinking about the great story Paul has laid out for us in the early chapters of Romans, affect the way you think about placing your life before God as an offering?

2.  It's important to note that our "offering" is not a payment. Christ's sacrifice on the cross was a gift, not a loan that needs repaid. (And that's good news, because we could never repay that debt!) It is instead a show of gratitude and an acknowledgement that everything we have—even the air we breathe—is a gift from God. Think of a time when you have given a gift to someone. How did they respond? Was their response a repayment? Did it need to be proportionate to the gift? (For instance, if you gave someone a $50 gift card and they responded with a sincere hug, is that "enough" or do they need to do more?) Does this change the way you look at your offering to the Lord?

# *Day 9*

## GOD HAS GIFTED YOU

**Read:** Romans 12:1-8

**Consider:**

In this passage, Paul tells his readers to present their lives as a living sacrifice to God, exhorts them to be humble, then encourages them to use their gifts. He is writing to a church that has become divided into Jews and non-Jews, who both think their way is the best way, so he reminds them that God has made them unique—with different gifts and abilities—so they can come together as one complete body.

Often we think of humility as being the opposite of embracing our gifts—that if we're truly humble, we will pretend that we aren't talented so no one thinks we are bragging. But Paul tells us to be humble *and* to recognize and use our gifts!

**Journal:**

1. What does it look like to humbly embrace the gifts God has given you?

2. How might Paul's words in these verses encourage unity in a divided church?

3. What are some of the ways God has gifted you?

# Day 10

## PART OF THE WHOLE

**Read:** 1 Corinthians 12:12-27

**Consider:**

Paul addresses both the individual and the united body here, showing the importance of both. We are each valued members of Christ's body—but we are also part of something much bigger than any one of us. Gaining this perspective reminds us to be humble and encourages us to embrace our worth.

We live in a highly individualistic society, and this carries over into our faith as well. We tend to think of our Christianity as being solely about the relationship between ourselves and God. And while that is important, we are not just called to a relationship with the Lord—we are called to life as part of a body of believers. God loves and has a purpose for each one of us, but ultimately he is building a family of restored people through Jesus.

**Journal:**

1. How does thinking of yourself as one part of a body change your perspective on your faith and your purpose in life?

2. In what ways have you let pride get in the way of helping to build up the body?

3. In what ways have your own insecurities prevent you from contributing to the body?

# USING YOUR GIFTS FOR THE BODY

**Read:** 1 Corinthians 12:12-27

**Consider:**

We often place more emphasis on gifts or characteristics that we consider to be of greater value than others. Paul reminds us here that every single part of the body is important and does necessary work. Not only that, but the various parts of the body need to work together—to utilize their gifts and abilities in conjunction with one another—in order for the whole body to function properly!

**Journal:**

1. What gifts or abilities do you have that you tend to downplay or think of as unimportant? What are some ways those abilities help the body of Christ? How might it hinder the body if you don't use them?

2. How can you better use your gifts in conjunction with others to help the body as a whole?

# Day 12

## IMPACT & IMPORTANCE

**Read:** 1 Corinthians 12:12-27

**Consider:**

It's easy to think our lives must be big to be significant—that we must have big accomplishments, wealth, or fame in order to matter. This passage tells a different story, though. Paul reminds us that even the parts of the body we think of as unimportant fill important roles. Take, for example, the eyelash. Talk about small! And does it even do anything? It seems so insignificant! But eyelashes protect our eyes from small particles of dust and dirt—and if you've ever had something in your eye, you know how distracting and debilitating that can be!

My friend, our lives do not have to be large to matter. You are a vital member of the body of Christ, and a cherished child of the King. God made you exactly as you are, he loves you exactly as you are, and he wants to use you exactly as you are. You matter. Your gifts and abilities matter. You are important.

**Journal:**

1.  Who are some of the people who have had the biggest impact on you? List 3-5 of the most influential people in your life. Are they celebrities? Did they impact you with their wealth and power? Or did they just show up and love you in just the right way at the right time?

2.  What can you do to serve the body of Christ right where you are today?

# WHAT WE BRING TO THE TABLE

**Read:** Ephesians 2:1-10

**Consider:**

Any time we want to know exactly how significant we are, this is a great passage to turn to. Verses 1-3 tell us what we bring to the table. Thank goodness Paul doesn't end there! Verses 4-9 remind us that it's not up to us. God is the one who has done the work.

**Journal:**

1. Reread verses 1-3 and make a list of all the ways it describes us. (It's not a pretty picture…!)

2. Now make a list of what verses 4-9 say about God. Looking at those lists side-by-side is pretty eye-opening, isn't it?

3. The beginning of this passage doesn't say we were weak or needed to work harder or needed to turn our lives around. It says we were dead. How does that change the way you look at earning your significance?

# Day 14

## GOD'S MASTERPIECE

**Read:** Ephesians 2:1-10

**Consider:**

Now we come to verse 10 with fresh eyes. Even though we are helpless and nothing without God, even though we can do nothing to earn our salvation, even though we were dead in our sins without him... He calls us his work-manship. The New Living Translation says, "We are God's masterpiece." Masterpiece! That is the kind of pride and joy he takes in us.

But there's more. He didn't just make us to display on the wall. He lovingly and carefully crafted us with gifts and abilities and experiences "for good works." Our works will never save us. We aren't meant to stack up accomplishments to curry favor with God. But we are still called (invited) to do good works in order that we can fulfill God's purpose for us. We don't do good works to earn his love, but out of the overflow of his love that is already ours!

**Journal:**

1. Do you think of yourself as a masterpiece? How does it feel to see that God views you this way?

2. Are you striving to earn God's love with your accomplishments? Or are you doing good works out of the overflow of his love?

# *Part 3*

## TRUSTING GOD FOR OUR STEPS

When we think of finding our purpose, we often think of 5-year plans, vision boards, and checklists. And by all means, friend, dream big dreams! But remember that we ultimately are not in control. Our purpose is not about creating a plan and making it happen. It's about trusting and honoring God no matter what comes our way.

# Day 15

## OUR PLANS & GOD'S PLAN

**Read:** Proverbs 16:1-4

**Consider:**

As I researched commentaries for this entry, one phrase popped up over and over: "Man proposes, God disposes." In other words, God has given us a mind and a will and a desire to plan, and he wants to us to them! But we also have to remember that he has the final say. Ultimately we are subject to him, and his plans will never be thwarted.

That doesn't mean that everything will go smoothly if we just pray about it first. (Wouldn't that be great, though?) In fact, in Acts 16 we find that even Paul didn't always get it right the first time (verses 6-10). But when we seek to follow the Lord, when we make our plans but continually give them back to him, we can know that he has a purpose and a plan for everything that comes our way.

**Journal:**

1.  Have you ever wanted something that you thought was fine, until God showed you that your heart was in the wrong place? How did God reveal the truth to you? What did you do in response? How could it have gone differently?

2.  Have you had a time when you were seeking to honor God and do what was right, and it still didn't turn out the way you thought or hoped? Looking back, can you see a way that God used that situation for good, whether in your life or someone else's?

3.  What are some plans you have right now? How can you make sure you are committing them to the Lord?

# Day 16

## NOW AND THEN

**Read:** Ecclesiastes 3:1-15

**Consider:**

When my kids were little, I felt like time was slipping away from me. People would encourage me to embrace the season I was in, that there would be time for other things later, but I constantly felt like I needed to do more. Time felt like a luxury I didn't have if I wanted to be significant!

When I read the opening lines of Ecclesiastes 3, though, I felt them washing relief over me. We have the gift of time, friend, and it's not always going to look the same. You might dream of building something big and beautiful, but now might be a time for tearing down something else God wants to clear out of your life first. You might prefer to be out of the spotlight, but right now God might be calling you to speak up. You might want your life to be marked by joy, but now might be the time to mourn. That's OK. Live the season God has you in, and keep planning for what's next. A new time will come.

Let me tell you a secret: No one can do it all—not all at once, and not if they want to do anything well! We all have to accept our limitations and our seasons. Sometimes that means saying no for now. But a no for now does not mean no forever.

And maybe you're reading this and thinking, "Actually, now is my time! This is my time to say yes! This is my season to build!" Fantastic! Run with that! And know that if/when this season comes to an end, that's OK, too.

God's purpose for us is not accomplish one Big Important Thing. He wants us to be faithful in following him through all of our shifting seasons.

**Journal:**

1. How has God led and used you in different seasons of your life?

2. How can you better embrace the season he has you in now?

3. What are some of your plans/dreams? Do you think now might be the time to take the next step in them, or do you need to set them aside for another season? Either way, take some time to plan and assess, either what your next steps are and when you want to do them, or set a date (3, 6, or maybe 12 months from now) for when you will take another look at your current season and whether you're ready to move forward.

_____

_____

_____

_____

_____

_____

_____

_____

_____

_____

_____

_____

_____

_____

_____

_____

_____

_____

## BE JOYFUL & DO GOOD

**Read:** Ecclesiastes 3:1-15

**Consider:**

As we look at the second half of this passage, we are reminded of just how big God is... and how very small we are. The writer reminds us that God established his plan before the beginning of time. Whatever he does endures forever. His plans cannot be thwarted. And we cannot fully understand everything he is doing.

In other words, God doesn't need us. But his gift to us is that he invites us to be co-laborers with him! No, we don't see the big picture that he does and we don't always understand what he is doing. But we can still live with joy, knowing that whatever we do, we do it for and with him. Our job is to be joyful and do good... everything else is God's job.

**Journal:**

1.  The writer encourages his reader to "take pleasure in all his toil." The words "pleasure" and "toil" don't seem like they belong in the same sentence! How can we take pleasure in our toil?

2.  Read verses 14 and 15 again. What do you think about the idea that nothing can be added to or taken away from what God does? Does that feel freeing or frustrating?

3.  As you think about the idea of seasons from yesterday and the lesson today, how does that affect the way you live today? How about your plans for the future? How can you "be joyful and do good" in your current season? What if your future plans don't come together the way you expected?

# Day 18

## DO IT WITH LOVE

**Read:** 1 Corinthians 13

**Consider:**

The message of verses 1-3 is clear: If we aren't acting out of love, it doesn't matter what we do. Remember, God cares far less about what you do than who you are. Before we focus too much on what our purpose is, we need to get our hearts in the right place. If we strive for our accomplishments to earn love and importance instead of acting out of love, we wind up feeling empty rather than fulfilled.

**Journal:**

1. How does it make you feel to know that if you do all the right things—if you do big and amazing things—but do them without love, you are *nothing* according to the passage? Have you ever experienced a time when you accomplished something big but felt empty afterward because you were looking to gain love/importance from your accomplishment instead of acting out of love?

2. Read the description of love in verses 4-8a. Are those words that describe you? You can try the old trick of inserting your name in place of the word love ("_____ is patient and kind; _____ does not envy or boast; _____ is not arrogant or rude" and so on). Does that sound accurate? If not, how can starting here help you to better live out your purpose?

# *Day 19*

## ALL THINGS WORK TOGETHER FOR GOOD

**Read:** Romans 8:18-30

**Consider:**

If we read verse 28 on its own, we are tempted to expect everything in life to go great if we just do all the right things… an attitude that will invariably end in disappointment. If we go back and start reading in verse 18, though, we'll see that Paul has been talking about finding hope in the midst of suffering. That is the context he brings to this passage. When he tells us that all things work together for good, he doesn't necessarily mean our earthly definition of good—at least, not in the short-term. He is talking more about the way a parent might tell a child, "I'm doing this for your own good." It doesn't always feel good while it's happening, but the end result is for a purpose.

**Journal:**

1.  How does reading this passage in its context reshape your understanding of verse 28?

2.  A former pastor of mine used to say, "God does all things for our good and his glory." When have you seen God use your own hard circumstances for your good? For his glory?

## CALLED ACCORDING TO HIS PURPOSE

**Read:** Romans 8:28-30

**Consider:**

Sometimes I read phrases like "called according to his purpose" and think, "Great, God! But what is your purpose?" But in verse 29, we learn exactly what his purpose for us is: "to be conformed to the image of his Son, in order that he might be the firstborn among many brothers." Read that again, friend. God's purpose for us is twofold:

1. That we look more and more like Christ

2. That we become members of—and help to grow—God's family.

God is calling us—inviting us—to be part of his family and look more like Christ. That is his purpose for us! And it gets better: it's something he is accomplishing in us! Verse 30 tells us that he called us, he justified us, and he glorified us. It's not our job to accomplish, it is our job to walk in what he has already done!

**Journal:**

1. How is God conforming you to the image of Christ?

2. How have you tried to earn your justification? How does it look different to stop striving for justification and instead walk in what God has already accomplished?

3. If this is the purpose we have been called to, do you feel like you are living out that purpose? If not, what do you think needs to change?

# *Part 4*

## KNOWING (AND LIVING) OUR PURPOSE

Finally! We are 2/3 of the way through this study, and we are finally ready to talk about what our purpose is! Hopefully by now you've started to realize that it might look a little different than you originally planned.

My friend, God absolutely has a purpose and a plan for you. He has uniquely gifted you. He has put you right where you are on purpose, for a purpose. But *your* purpose—God's individual plan for your life—is a subset of *our* purpose. He has given all of his followers, his family, a mission. And when we are living that out, that is when we will feel the joy and satisfaction of a life lived on purpose, no matter what we're doing. Even in the midst of our everyday, ordinary lives.

# Day 21

## GLORIFY GOD & ENJOY HIM FOREVER

**Read:** Psalm 150

**Consider:**

This simple psalm pretty much sums up our purpose: praise the Lord! The Westminster catechism teaches, "The chief end of man is to glorify God and enjoy him forever." This is it, friend! Whatever else we do, we are created to bring glory to God! I love that the psalmist lists all different instruments, including "loud clashing cymbals"—it's like he's saying, "Look, even if you have no other talents, you can just bang stuff together. Just do whatever you can to praise God."

**Journal:**

1. Verse 2 tells us to praise God for what he does ("his mighty deeds") and who he is ("his excellent greatness"). Spend some time writing down praises for each of those categories. (For example, I can praise God for the prayers he has answered in my life—his deeds—and also thank him for being all-knowing, all-powerful, the Beginning and the End—who he is.)

2. We often think of praise in terms of music, just like the psalmist describes here. How else can we praise God in our lives? (Hint: Go back to Day 7 when we talked about Romans 12:1.)

3. What are some other ways you can "enjoy God" in your life?

# Day 22

## WHAT DOES THE LORD REQUIRE OF ME?

**Read:** Micah 6:6-8

**Consider:**

Although the exact terms might be different, Micah here expresses the longing of all of our hearts: "God, what can I possibly offer you that will be enough? How can I do anything worthy of you?" While we might not think about burnt offerings and sacrifices, the idea is the same… nothing we do or give could ever be enough. But God isn't looking for gifts. He doesn't want us to impress him. (Which is good news, because we can't.) God is after our hearts—that we do justice, love kindness, and walk humbly with him.

**Journal:**

1. How have you tried to earn God's favor in the past?

2. Have you ever felt proud, like you deserved God's love because you were accomplishing so much? Have you ever felt humble, like Micah mentions in this passage, like you could never possibly do enough?

3. Think about the attributes God extols here: justice, kindness, and humility. Are those attributes someone would use to describe you? Where do you think you need to focus/grow?

## FOLLOW JESUS' EXAMPLE

**Read:** John 13:12-17, 33-35

**Consider:**

Today's passages come from the Last Supper, Jesus's final night with his disciples. He knows what is coming, and he knows this is his last chance to impress upon them the most important aspects of everything he wants them to know. And he begins by *washing their feet*. Then, once their minds have been blown by this act of humility, he tells them that this wasn't just an act of kindness—it was an example for them to follow. They are to serve one another—and again, in verse 33, he commands them to love one another. Remember that he is speaking to a group of men who all follow him. His command here is not for them to love the world, but fellow believers.

I'm not at all saying we aren't supposed to love the whole world. I am simply saying that, in order for the world to see what Jesus is all about, they need to first see us loving and serving our family in Christ.

**Journal:**

1. Think of a time someone "washed your feet" so to speak—when has someone served you or loved you in a sacrificial way?

2. How can you follow Jesus's example of humility and love to other believers? Do you think you are setting an example of love for those around you?

# Day 24

## ABIDE IN CHRIST

**Read:** John 15:1-17

**Consider:**

If we want to live fruitful lives, we must abide in Christ. In fact, he warns us, "apart from me you can do nothing." He is our vine—our source of life—and we must draw from him in order bear fruit in our lives. The word for "abide" here means to dwell—to dig in and live there. It isn't a passive thing that just happens. It takes intentionality. But the good news is that Jesus also promises, "Abide in me, and I in you." This is not a one-sided relationship! He will pour his life and love into us, and we can reinvest it right back into our relationship with him!

**Journal:**

1. What does it look like to "abide" or "dwell" in Christ?

2. What kind of fruit should we be looking for in our lives?

3. Have you experienced times of abundance and times of drought/famine in your walk with the Lord? What did those look like? What led you out of the drought season?

4. When you are abiding in Christ, how does that overflow into your life? How does/could it make you more purposeful?

# *Day* 25

## A NEW COMMANDMENT

**Read:** John 15:1-17

**Consider:**

Jesus gives us a clear path to follow in these verses, but he does it in a sort of backwards way. He starts with the end goal, then tells us how to get there.

End goal: Abiding in him.

How: Obeying his commandments (verse 10).

What he is commanding us to do: Love one another as he has loved us (verse 12).

We abide in him by loving each other—and not just by being nice, but by loving sacrificially. In fact, he tells his disciples this on the very same night that he humbled himself and washed their feet. That example must still be in their minds, seeing their Master kneeling before them, scrubbing away the dirt and grime like a lowly servant. And his next act of love, the one they still didn't see coming, would be to die for them!

We are called to love one another as Christ has loved us. For most of us, that doesn't mean we literally have to lay down our lives for others, but it does mean setting aside our pride and loving sacrificially.

**Journal:**

1.  What does it mean to love as Christ loves you?

2.  What are some specific ways you can better love those around you today?

3.  How can we love sacrificially while maintaining boundaries to keep ourselves healthy? Are there relationships in your life that might require you to think through some specific boundaries?

*Day 26*

# PETER'S MISSION (AND OURS)

**Read:** John 21:15-22

**Consider:**

This is such a beautiful picture of how Jesus restores those he loves. Peter had denied Jesus three times, just as Jesus had predicted. If I were Peter, my stomach would have been in knots every time I saw the resurrected Christ. He had wanted so badly to be Jesus's most devoted follower... but he had completely dropped the ball. How long until Jesus decided to scold him? Could Peter even continue as a disciple, or had his failure completely disqualified him?

But when Jesus addresses Peter, it isn't with words of disappointment and frustration. He asks Peter (three times—did you catch that?) if he loves him. This isn't because Jesus was unsure, but because he wanted Peter to hear the affirmation coming from his own lips. And then he doesn't tell Peter, "OK, then here's what you need to do to get your life back on track." He gives him a mission—starting immediately. And his mission? To love others.

Start right now, right where you are.

**Journal:**

1. When have you felt disqualified from serving God because of your mistakes?

2. Do you have sin standing between you and the Lord today? Take a moment to confess and repent, and let his healing forgiveness restore your heart.

3. Peter denied Christ three times as Jesus was being beaten and prepared to die on the cross. And yet, he wasn't disqualified from service! On the contrary, he is regarded as a pillar of the faith! How does this change your perspective on how your own past failures impact your ability to serve God?

# WHAT ABOUT HIM (OR HER)?

**Read:** John 21:15-22

**Consider:**

After Jesus has a heartfelt one-on-one with Peter, he entrusts his disciple with some important but uncomfortable information: Peter would be martyred for his faith. The same Peter who denied his Master would eventually stand up for him to the point of death. It's hard to imagine the intimacy of this moment.

Instead of being drawn to his Savior, though, Peter is distracted. He is distracted by the solemnity of the news and by the other disciple (John) he sees lurking nearby. "What about him?" he asks Jesus. Maybe he's feeling a little self-pity and wondering, "Does John have to be killed for you, too?" Or perhaps the question was prideful: "What about this beloved disciple of yours, Jesus? Will he be strong and courageous enough to be martyred for you?"

But don't miss Jesus's response here: "If it is my will that he remain until I come, what is that to you? *You follow me*" (verse 22, emphasis added). Don't you just love it when Jesus gets a little sassy and sarcastic? Jesus basically tells Peter, "You know what? That's none of your business. My plan for John is my plan for John. You just stay in your lane, Peter."

Comparison is a dangerous trap, my friend. When we get caught up worrying about what God is doing in someone else's life, we forget to look at the One who is guiding our steps. He's got a plan for each one of us, and here it is: "You follow me."

**Journal:**

1. Do you ever struggle with comparison? Where have you seen it pop up in your life?

2. "Comparison is the thief of joy." –Theodore Roosevelt. How has comparison stolen from you? Has it ever kept you from accomplishing

something God has put before you? Has it kept you from experiencing joy in the things you have accomplished?

3. Comparison seems to come into play even more when we are struggling, just like Peter wanting to deflect from the hard news Jesus had given him. How can you create healthy boundaries and triggers to help you stop comparison in its tracks?

# Day 28

## CALLING: AN INVITATION TO *COME*

**Read:** Matthew 4:18-22

**Consider:**

In our Christian culture, we worry a lot about our calling—what it is, how we find it, what if we miss it. But in the Bible, the word used for calling is *klēsis*, which literally means "to invite." And that's exactly what we see here. When Jesus calls his first disciples, he invites them to follow him. And here's the best part: He doesn't tell them he'll *teach* them how to be fishers of men. He doesn't say, "I want you to *learn* to fish for men." He says, "I will *make* you fishers of men." He does the transformative work! Our job is to do exactly what the men in this passage do: follow him.

**Journal:**

1. How would you have defined the word "calling" before reading this entry? How does looking at calling as an invitation change your perspective?

2. How have you seen God transform you as you follow him?

# Day 29

## CALLING: A COMMAND TO GO

**Read:** Matthew 28:16-20

**Consider:**

When Jesus met the disciples, he invited them to *come*, to follow him. Now as he gets ready to depart, he commands them to *go*. He charges them—and us—to make disciples. It might sound a little scary at first, especially if we aren't pastors or we're not comfortable just approaching people on the street to tell them about Jesus. But there is more to being a disciple maker than those overt acts. In fact, every one of us has disciples. Who are you influencing? Who looks up to you, listens to you? You are making disciples of those people... but who or what are you pointing them to? What are you teaching them?

**Journal:**

1. Start with the questions listed above. Who are you influencing in your life? Who looks up to you, listens to you?

2. Who or what are you pointing your "disciples" to? When they look at your life, do they see Jesus?

3. How else can you live out this great commission to make disciples?

# THE GREATEST COMMANDMENT

**Read:** Matthew 22:34-40

**Consider:**

We are not the first generation to wonder what it is that God wants us to do. Our desire to have exact next steps goes back to the beginning of time. In fact, the Israelites were so intent on doing the right thing that they took God's laws and started adding to them. At the time of Jesus, some of the most devout Jews would literally take out a tenth of their spices each week to give back to God.

Unfortunately, when we get too focused on our actions, we often forget that God is actually far more concerned with our hearts. Jesus reminds us here that a life of following God is less about doing the right things than about the state of our hearts. If we want to live a life of purpose, it starts here, with the greatest commandment: "Love the Lord your God with all your heart and with all your soul and with all your mind... And a second is like it: You shall love your neighbor as yourself" (37 & 39).

In fact, Jesus goes on to say, "On these two commandments depend all the Law and the Prophets" (40). In other words, friend, **this is the key**! If we don't get this part right, everything else falls apart!

**Journal:**

1.  Read Deuteronomy 6:4-5, the passage Jesus is referencing for the first commandment. Take a few minutes to think about each of the areas mentioned here. How do we love God with our hearts? How do we love him with our souls? How do we love him with our might? In our society, we tend to think of love as purely an emotion, but the Bible seems to imply it is more than a feeling.

2.  How can we love our neighbor as ourselves? Why are those last two words included—how is that different from simply loving our neighbor?

# BRINGING IT ALL TOGETHER

Yes, I know, it's supposed to be 30 days, not 31. But I think we could use an extra day just to reflect on what we've learned, don't you? Spend a few minutes looking back through this journal. What passages stand out to you? Reread them. Reread your notes and journal entries for those days. Just take a few minutes remember what God has done as you prepare to head out into the next moments, days, weeks, and years of your life with purpose.

**Journal:**

1. Go back to Day 1 and think about your expectations for this journal. What did you hope to gain? What did you gain? How has your idea of purpose changed? How has it solidified?

2. What next steps can and will you take in living a life of purpose?

*Appendix 1*

# HOW TO STUDY THE BIBLE

Few things in my life have been more rewarding than learning how to truly study the Bible for myself. Meditating on God's Word, digging into the context and meaning of the passages, and applying them to my life has given a new depth and richness to my relationship with Jesus. Don't get me wrong—I love a good Bible study and gleaning from other Bible teachers and Christians. But we should always bring what we learn back to God and His Word for ourselves. I am thankful for the chance to share a few of my favorite tips with you. So grab a pen, a notebook, and your Bible (or Bible app of choice!), and let's start studying!

(Some of these steps will also be in the *Using this Journal* section, but I want to list them again here in case you utilize this appendix when you are doing other studies.)

## Pray

Begin by inviting the Holy Spirit to open the truth of God's Word to you. Focus your mind on the Lord and let go of distractions. Praise and worship God. Confess any sin that might be creating a barrier. Ask him to open your eyes to what he wants you to learn as you study.

## Read

Read and re-read the passage. Take a look at it in a few different translations. (See Bible Study Resources for more information.) Pick one or two verses and write them out. You can copy them exactly or paraphrase them in your own words.

**Observe**

Write down observations about the passage. Answer the basic questions:

- Who wrote this?
- To whom was it written?
- When was it written?
- What does it say? (Write a few sentences to summarize the main idea.)
- Why was it written? (What was happening in the world and/or with the audience?)
- How does this passage fit into the whole of the book? How does it fit into God's big story of creation -> fall -> redemption -> renewal?

Also, look for repeated words or words that jump out at you. Consider making a list or chart of what you learn in the text.

Spend some time here! This is the part we want to run past, but it sets the stage for everything else! Make sure you really dig into what God's Word says before you start trying to pull out meaning and application.

**Interpret**

At this stage, you can begin to look beyond the few verses you are studying. You may want to glance over the whole chapter or think about the theme of the book to get a feel for the context (if you didn't already in the observation stage). Look up any cross-references that go along with the passage. Study the key/repeated words you noted in your observations. Consult a commentary. (See Bible Study Resources if you're not sure how to start on these.) Try to answer these questions:

- What does this passage teach me about God (his character, his deeds, his plan for the world)?
- What would this have meant to the original audience?

## Apply

What did the author intend for the reader to do/believe as a result of this passage? Was there a call to action—or a call to cease something? An instruction for life? What action can you take as a result of what you learned about God and yourself? Make a plan for what you will do, when you will do it, and how you will do it. Be specific.

## Pray

Yes, again. Pray a portion of the Scripture back to God. Praise him for His Word that is living and active. Ask him for his strength and power to live out what you have learned.

# *Appendix 2*

# BIBLE STUDY RESOURCES

All kinds of exhaustive Bible study resource lists abound on the internet. They are incredibly useful but can also be overwhelming. Full of Bible dictionaries, commentaries, atlases, interlinear Bibles, study Bibles, and so much more, those lists have great information—but if you start there, you may give up before you ever begin!

I'm not telling you that to scare you, but to reassure you. It's OK to start small. You don't even have to have your own Bible. You can absolutely use apps and websites! Honestly, I do recommend that you have a physical Bible of your own to touch and make notes in and highlight and underline—but if you don't have that right now, don't let it stop you! As far as translations, I personally like the ESV, and I grew up with the NIV, which is also great. While I really like using paraphrases like The Message to help me get a new perspective on familiar passages, I don't recommend that as your primary text. A word-for-word or phrase-for-phrase translation (again, like the ESV or NIV) will be the most accurate representation of God's Word.

Once you have a good Bible text, a few extra tools can help you to go deeper into your study. Below are just a few of the resources I keep close by when I am studying the Bible. For more of my recommendations, go to my website: KatyEpling.com/resources.

**Bible Gateway** – Free website/app that provides many translations of the Bible, as well as devotionals and reading plans.

**You Version** – Free website/app that provides many translations of the Bible, as well as devotionals and reading plans.

**Blue Letter Bible** – Free website/app for deeper Bible study. Users can input a specific verse and see it broken down word-by-word, see the meaning of the original Hebrew/Greek, and study its use throughout the Bible in the concordance. Blue Letter Bible also provides commentaries, reference materials (dictionaries, concordances, timelines, etc), and devotionals.

*Women of the Word* by Jen Wilkin – An excellent book that outlines both how to study the Bible and why it is important to study it well. Jen also walks readers step-by-step through the process she outlines. This book has been a huge help to me!

# ABOUT THE AUTHOR

Katy Epling is a writer and speaker in northeast Ohio. The author of *Finding Jesus: A Christmas Devotional*, Katy loves to help others root their identity in Christ. Katy has made it her mission to live on purpose, for a purpose—and to encourage everyone she encounters to do the same. Her writing has been featured on sites such as *The Huffington Post, Today Parents, The Mighty, Her View From Home,* and *Relevant Magazine.*

Katy and her husband Jon have three beautiful children who provide her with never-ending material, both dramatic and comedic. When she isn't writing or speaking, she can be found packing lunches, folding laundry, and making dinner. (And on rare occasions, sipping a chai latte with a friend.) You can find her online at katyepling.com, on Facebook (facebook.com/katyepling), and on Instagram (instagram.com/katyepling).

Made in the USA
Coppell, TX
24 January 2021